Martin Bruckner

AN iLLUSTRATED BOOK OF
BIG THOUGHTS
FROM LiTTLE KiDS

WORKMAN PUBLISHING • NEW YORK

Library of Congress Cataloging-in-Publication Data is available.

ISBN 978-0-7611-8914-5

Design by Ariana Abud

Workman books are available at special discounts when purchased in bulk for premiums and sales promotions as well as for fund-raising or educational use. Special editions or book excerpts also can be created to specification. For details, contact the Special Sales Director at the address below, or send an email to specialmarkets@workman.com.

Workman Publishing Co., Inc.
225 Varick Street
New York, NY 10014-4381
workman.com

WORKMAN is a registered trademark of Workman Publishing Co., Inc.

Printed in China
First printing March 2017

10 9 8 7 6 5 4 3 2 1

♥
for Michelle
and
Harper

The Story of "Spaghetti Toes"

My daughter, Harper, has requested the same dinner every single night since she started solid foods: "nooles" (noodles), no exceptions or substitutions. Being parents who have learned to pick our battles, my wife, Michelle, and I have accepted the fact that a big bowl of spaghetti, macaroni and cheese, or ramen will be on our dinner table more nights than not.

One evening in particular, Harper, being a two-year-old, had lost interest in eating the noodles and instead was playing with them. My wife wasn't having any of it, and what I heard next is a phrase that I will never forget: "Please don't put spaghetti between your toes." I couldn't believe my ears. I was as equally humored as I was disgusted. But an idea slithered into my brain just as the noodles had slithered between my daughter's toes.

Being an artist by profession, my first thought was: "that would make for a funny piece of artwork." As time went on and as Harper explored the English language, hilarious phrases became an ever present part of our daily lives, coming from all three of us. I soon began a daily regimen of doodling as many of them as I could.

When Mother's Day rolled around, I decided to take a small collection of these newly illustrated musings and put them into a little book for my wife. She loved it, so I threw it out on the Internet and it quickly turned into something that would change all of our lives forever.

After the awesome people behind Pleated-Jeans.com helped our family's antics go viral, I started to help other parents memorialize the sayings of their own child philosophers, geniuses, and comedians. My wife had a small, yet thriving, shop on Etsy, so we added a Custom Quote listing and have been translating children's wacky, gross, weird, and hilarious sayings into art ever since.

Here I am proud to present a compilation of the wackiest, grossest, weirdest, and most accidentally hilarious wisdom, said by children (including my own, of course) and drawn by me.

—Martin Bruckner
Spaghetti-Toes.com

I Like You some days, Mom.

Charlotte, age 3,
made this claim
upon waking her
mom one morning.

CUDDLING MAKES ME HUNGRY.

I Don't
WANT TO Be aN
ASTroNAUT ANYMORE.
I WaNT to bE
the girL WHo TURNs
the LiGHts ON.

Katie, age 4, discovered
that the hand position
for "I love you" in sign
language can be easily
flipped to shoot strands
of spider web out of
the wrist.

You're Rich And Cruel.

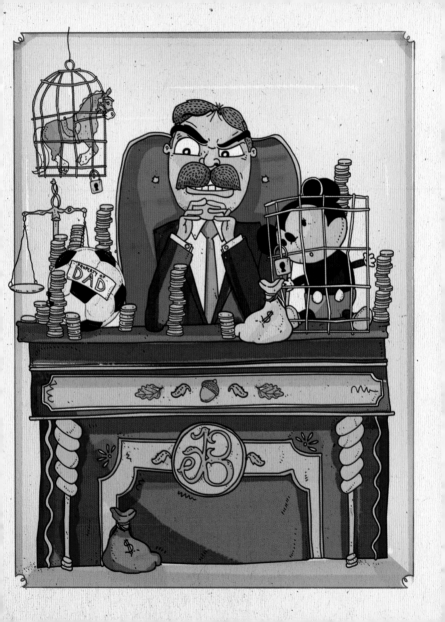

VOLCANOES
are the
EARTH'S BUTT.
That's HOW
the EARTH
gets THE
GAS OUT!

DON'T LICK YOUR BOSS.

Corrina, age 5, prefers "Olly olly booya" to the more traditional version: "Hallelujah."

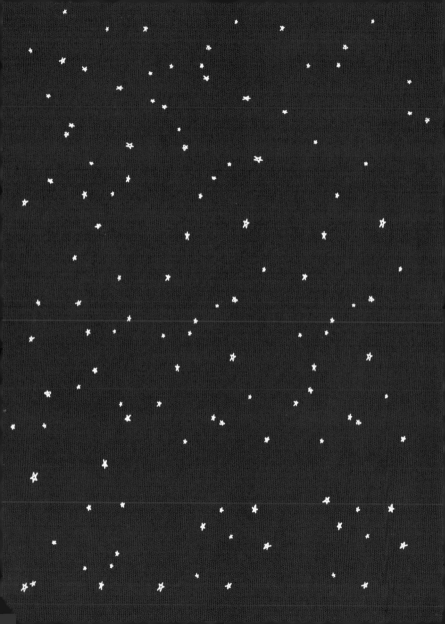

you're the
BEST WORLD,
DAD!

Will you please

respect My
Apology?

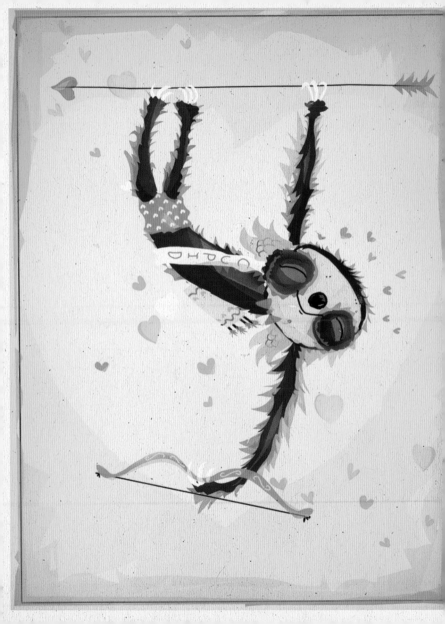

Harper Grace, age 3

Dad: Harper, do you know who Cupid is?

Harper: Um, some sort of sloth or something?

Dad: Uh...

EMPIRE SNAKE BUILDING

I'm a cheetah.
Daddy's a cheetah.
Ella's a cheetah.

Mommy's a grassland goat.

i love you with my heart and soil.

MY CLOTHES WERE TOO TIGHT TO PLAY WITH MY TRAINS.

I ♥ TRAI

dear
GOD,

Harper Grace, age 3

One night, when her mom was attempting to make dinner, Harper began circling on all fours in the kitchen.

Mom: Harper, what are you doing?

Harper: I'm training to be a wolf!

Emma, age 4

Emma: Is dang-it a bad word?

Mom: Well, there are definitely worse words.

Emma: Like stupid? Or a**hole?

Mom: Um, yes, definitely worse.

ThEre aRe two PeoPLe wHo I Love SO Much and tHey woRk hARd For Me and give ME toys And make Me So HaPPy.

YOU
KNOW WHO?

SANTA

and

tHe

EASTeR

BUNNY.

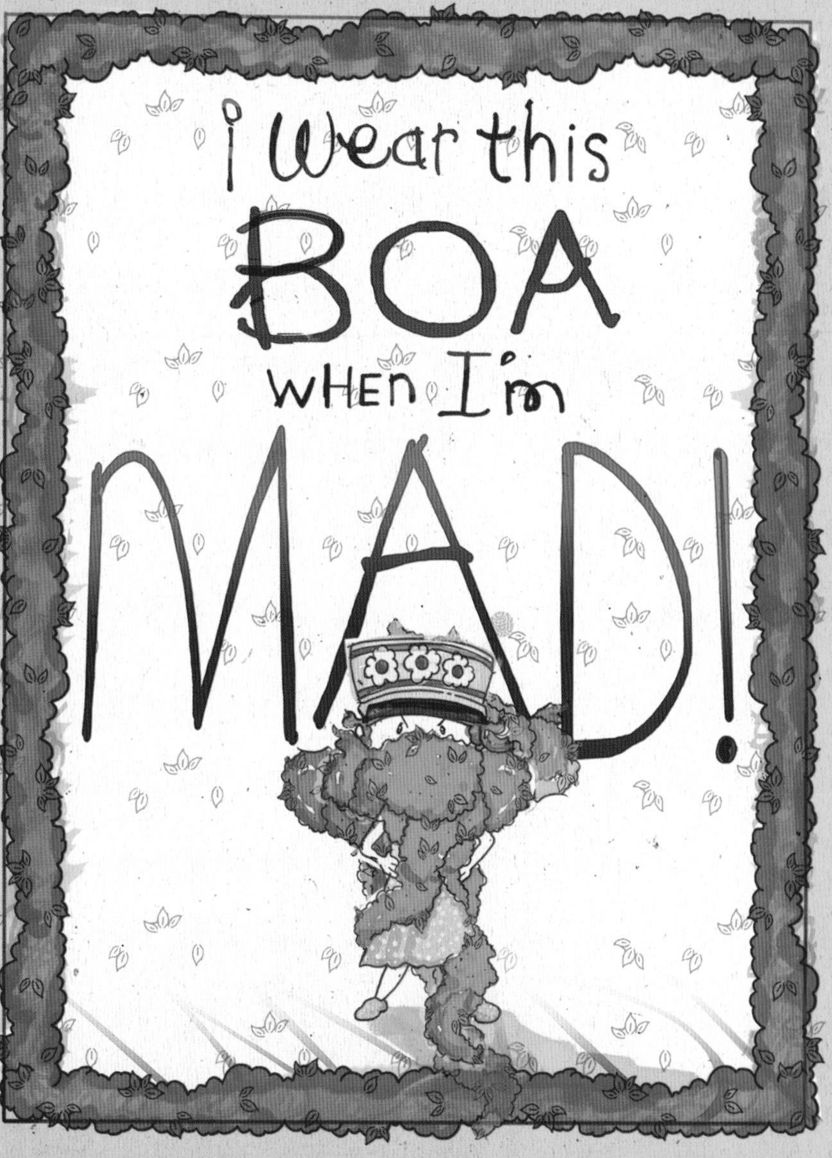
i wear this
BOA
WHEN I'm
MAD!

Cale, age 4, in response
to the question: "What
is the moral of the Adam
and Eve story?"

DADDY,
I LOVE YOU
PAST THE MOON
AND MARS
AND ALL
THE STARS
WHERE THERE'S
NOTHING.

I
LOVE
YOU
WHERE
THERE'S
NOTHING.

AM I the
TOoth Fairy's
LATESt victim?

Bird,

get down.

Madison, age 1

Madison and her mom were outside standing in front of a big oak tree. Madison was watching a bird on the ground, just a few feet away. The bird cocked its head to look at her and abruptly flew into the tree, prompting Madison to blurt out, "Bird, get down." It was her very first sentence.

WATCH OUT FOR THE SHEEPS.

Sarah, age 3

Sarah has been cheerfully sending her father off
to work with this warning every day for about
a year, despite the fact that there is no chance
he would ever come across any sheep—or any
livestock at all, for that matter—on his commute.

WE ARE
NINJAS.

WE ARE NINJAS
WHO
LOOK
BOTH
WAYS
FOR
CARS.

WE ARE
SAFETY
NINJAS!

GOD IS GREAT.
GOD IS GREAT.

Meekie, age 4

Meekie, who was generally well-behaved, decided he would like to become a wild animal in the grocery store, terrorizing everyone in his path.

So his mom abandoned her shopping cart (you know it's bad when a mom abandons a cart full of groceries) and took him back to the car to go home.

Finally, they pulled into the driveway. Before his mom could turn around, Meekie said, "Whoa, hold on for a second, Mommy—are you still wearing your angry eyebrows?"

MOMMY,
I LOVE YOU
MORE THAN THE
DEVIL.

gummy Bears aren't alive, so they won't scream.

Frank, age 4, in a very matter-of-fact tone, as he was about to take his first bite of chocolate ice cream with gummy bears.

I'M
GONNA
MARRY YOU,
Mama!
ANd
I'M GONNA
Give YOU
A
pink
SpaRKLy
Race
Car.

WHEN I'M 29, I'LL FLY TO THE MOON...

THEN I'LL TRY THE SOUP.

I LOVE YOU A GOOGOLPLEX TIMES INFINITY

After she's finished crying, Darcy, age 3, often declares her need for a tissue with these words, in an Elmer Fudd-esque speech pattern.

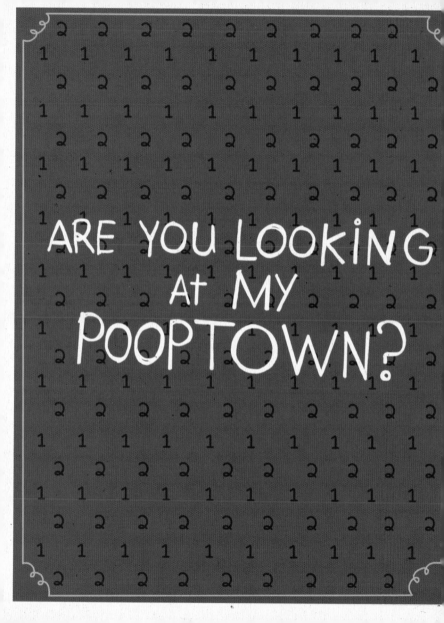

Laura, age 5

One snowy winter afternoon, Laura and her
Aunt Janie went sledding.

They came to a hill with two paths, where
Janie explained that one of the paths was more
treacherous than the other (there had been a few
serious injuries to sledders), so they would be
taking the safer route.

Laura considered this and came back with a
question: "Janie, how come I am full of courage
and you are full of worries?"

MOMMy, I thiNK
I Am totaLLy
IN LOVE WiTH yOU,
At leASt UNTiL
Dad GEtS HoME.

If we TRiEd to give OUR CAT A MUSTACHe, he WOULd PRObably nEVER TRust us aGAIN.

COWS can't GO
ON aIRPLANes.

Daddy,
I just Love
your
belly button.
It's so deep
a fairy
could
live
in
there.

Stephen, age 3½, made this observation upon meeting his baby sister for the first time.

BRUSHING WITH BARBIE LEGS GETS THE WORMS OUT.

Crumbs just follow me.

Haley, age 3

Haley had been covering the floor with evidence of her breakfast.

Mom: Haley, what a mess!

Haley: [shrugs] Crumbs just follow me.

Dark FADER
and the
STRONG POOPERS
ADMISSION 5 DRUGGATS
LIVE FROM MOS EISLEY CANTINA
ONE NIGHT ONLY
SP
SP
SP

MOMMY,

You Are my PLUM,
and you Are my PICKLE.

It sure is
FROGGY
Out.

I PUT ALL MY
CLOTHES IN THE DIRTY
CLOTHES HAMPSTER.

Laura, age 2

When her mother's back was turned mixing up some bread dough, Laura thought it would be the right moment to begin playing in the big bag of flour. Her mom soon turned around to discover a very dusty child and floor.

Mom: Laura, do you want a spanking?

Laura: No, I not done being bad yet!

I've been a LOT OF
Places, but
inside the BOX
ain't ONE of THEm!

Patrick, age 5,
announces this
mournfully after getting
in trouble, as though
his alter ego is the one
misbehaving.

Harper Grace, age 3

The on-again, off-again relationship that
Harper has with Spiderman took a turn
for the serious when she announced this
warning to her mother . . . while wearing her
dress-up wedding gown.

CAN YOU
HAND ME A
TENNIS
SHOE?

WHEN UNICORNS HATCH FROM THEIR EGGS,
THEY LOOK LIKE HORSES.

THEY GROW UP TO BE UNICORNS
AFTER THEY GROW THEIR CORN.

Jude, age 3½

Jude: I'm going to turn into a superhero!

Mom: Really? Which one?

Jude: Spicyguy!

what kind of ship do we have?
Friendship or Momship?

i'm practicing my Beetle Position

HOW TO DO A PROPER BEETLE POSITION

SIT DOWN AND RELAX.

STRETCH YOUR HAMSTRINGS.

BRING YOUR KNEES UP TO YOUR CHEST.

TIGHTLY SQUEEZE YOUR LEGS WITH YOUR ARMS. ROCK BACK + FORTH AND LET YOUR WHOLE BODY BE OVERCOME WITH PARANOIA.

Astraea, age 5, was found
curled up under the
dining table.

Mommy, I Love You so much in your beautiful pink and sparkly heart.

Mom, you follow Rowan.
Rowan, you follow me.

And I'm going to
follow my heart.

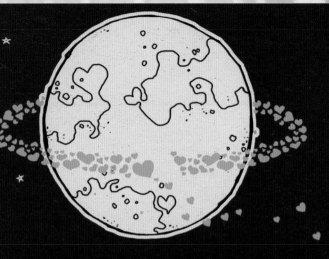

I LOVE
YOU
ALL THE
WAY TO
PLANET
DORF.

OR IS IT
JUST a
WORD?

I'M NOT BOSSY.

I'M A LEADER!

What
does
it
mean
to
"fall
in
LOVE"?

do you
FALL,
and
Love
is on
the
ground?

151

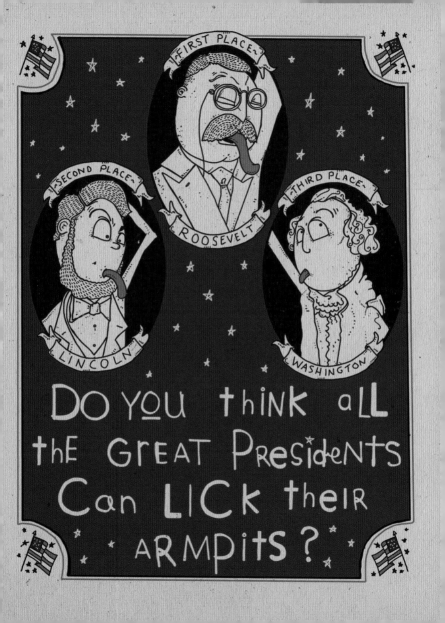

Mommy, your hair is nice and soft, just like a Raccoon.

ARe aNGels ReaL?

IS GrAndpa tHE NaME Of AN ANGel?

Gabriel, age 5

One night, Gabriel was eating dinner with his grandparents. His grandpa, who is Catholic, told him that Gabriel was the name of an angel. This prompted more questions.

Gabriel: Are angels real?

Grandpa: Yes, Gabriel.

Gabriel: Is Grandpa the name of an angel?

THAT MAKES
ME A LITTLE NERVOUS.

Harper, age 3, in one of
a series of heartbreaking
sentences said to her mother.

MOMMY,
i DON'T NEED
   YOUR MOUTH TO
TaLK TO ME
   RiGHT NOW.

I can't have milk...

GO BACK TO YOUR COW!!

MILK, MILK, GO AWAY!!!

MILK

166

Madison, age 7

Madison went through a period of being very concerned about chemicals and their negative effects on health. At roughly the same time, she developed a nervous sleeve-chewing habit. One day in art class, she dipped her sleeve in paint and chewed it—some got in her mouth. Panicking, she walked right up to the teacher and asked, "Is paint poisonous?"

The teacher's reply: "Only if you eat it."

When Madison came home crying, her mom immediately asked her what was wrong, prompting her to say, "I thought today was going to be my last day."

it's OK, DAddy—
MOMMY'S GOT LOTS
OF MONEY.

MOM, WHEN WE GO to HEAVEN, CAN I hold YOUR HAND?

Harper Grace, age 3

Harper's on-again, off-again romances have included turbulent relationships with Spiderman, Captain America, and Robin (green pants and elf slippers included). However, this time, the heartbreak was over a real person.

The pony-tailed janitor at the mall wouldn't marry her.

MY HEART doesn't Feel WELL.

my Princess is home.

My dinner
tummy is full,

Like
Sometimes

i
think

LEAfs
are
CHickens.

Mommy, do you

and Blankie

PLAY TOGether

while
I'm
at
School?

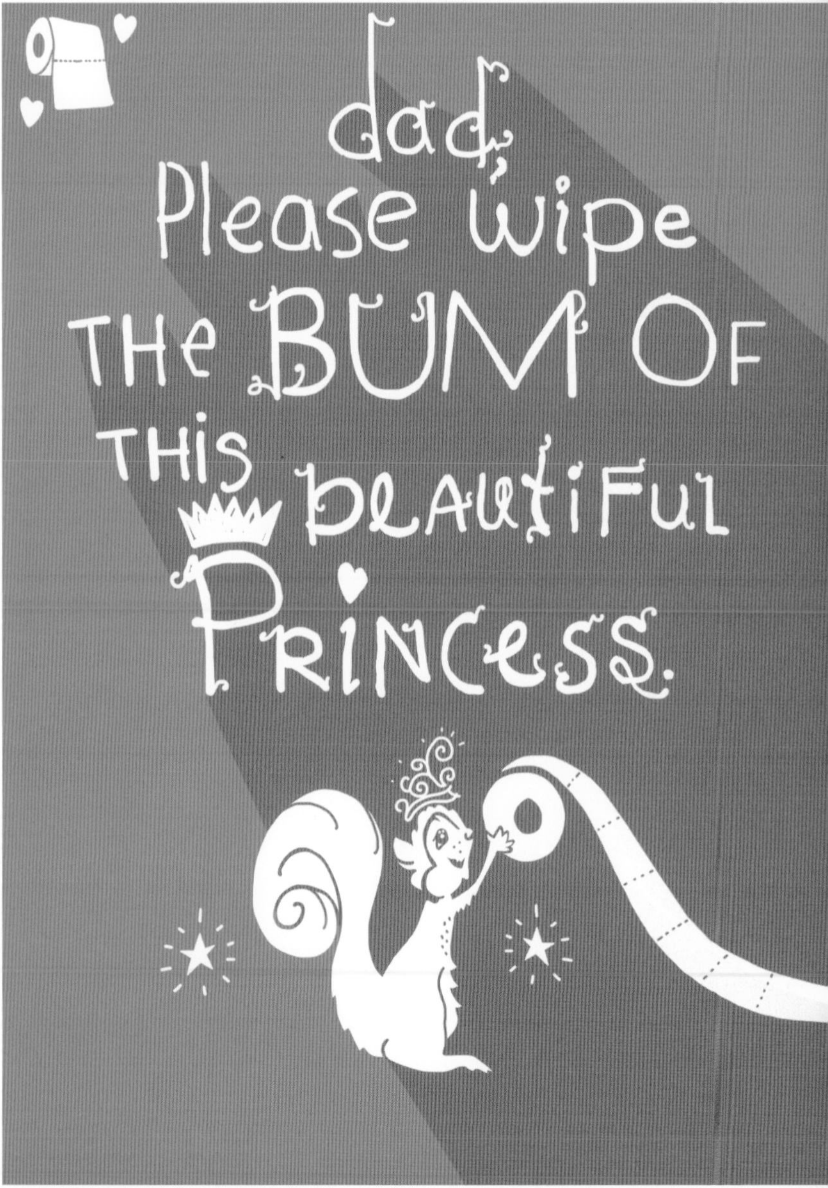
dad,
Please wipe
THE BUM OF
THIS beautiful
PRINCESS.

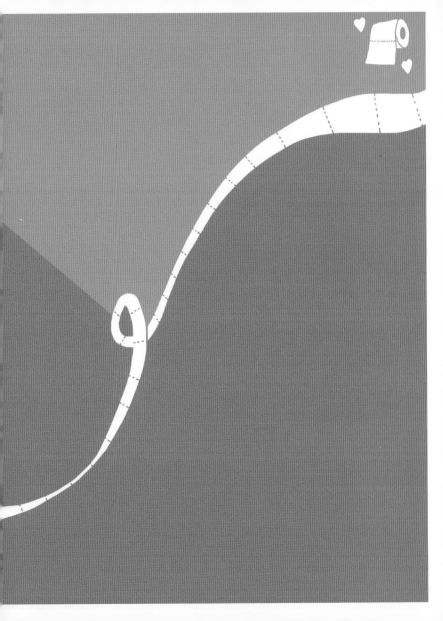

PiLLOW

FiGHTER

THE OnLy KInd OF zuCChini I LIke iS POPCorn.

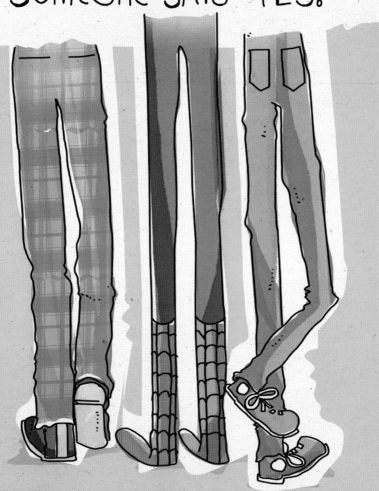

God has a big brown Beard that touches the ground, black socks, a big white shirt, one red shoe and one black shoe, and green pants. He's 87.

I don't HAVE
A yaWn yet.

pat-a-cake, pat-A-Cake,

Bake your men.

Joel, age 4, was sitting in his parents' bed, looking curiously at his dad's arm, when he made this inquiry about hair.

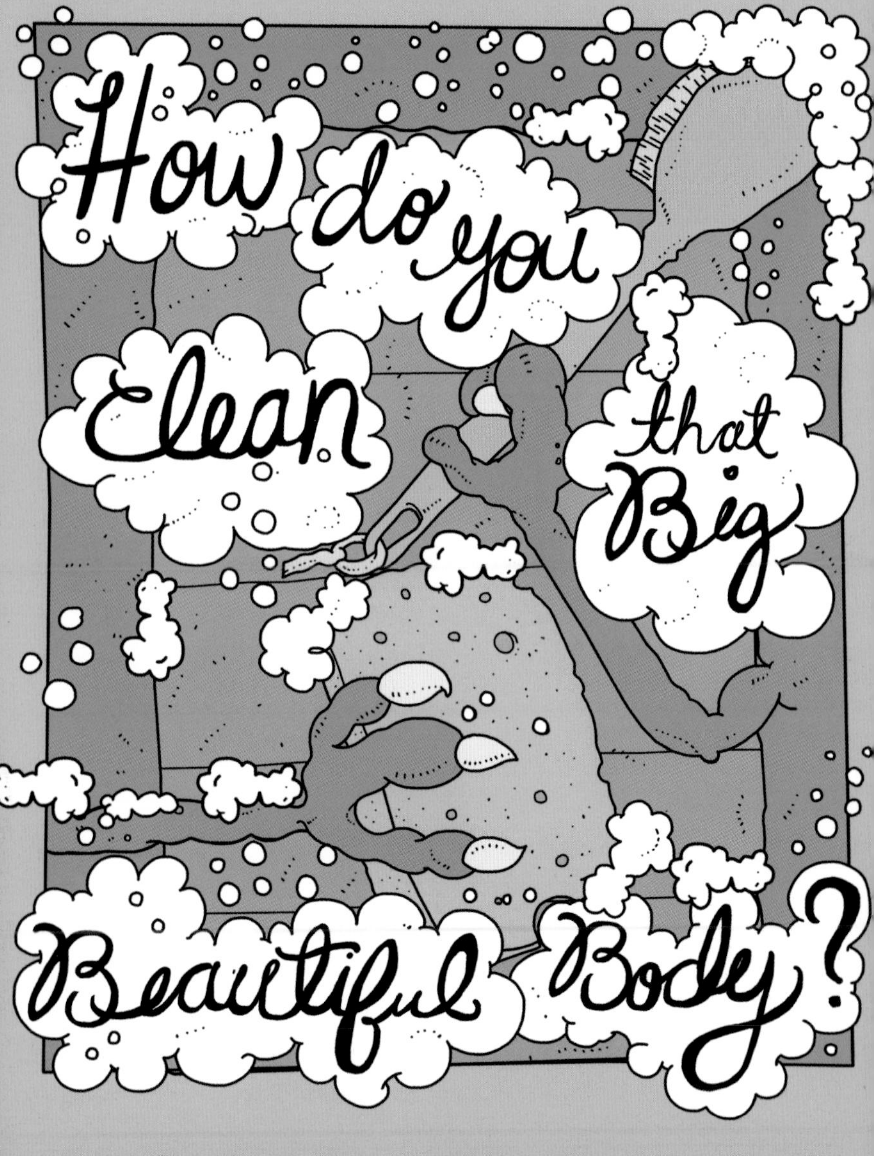
How do you
Clean that Big
Beautiful Body?

Gabi and Hailey, age 3

Gabi (always so polite and well-mannered) and her twin sister Hailey (the complete opposite) were going to the restroom with their fully grown older cousin Crystal, taking turns going to the potty, when the following dialogue ensued.

Gabi: Crystal, can I ask you a question?

Crystal: Absolutely.

Gabi, with amazement and wonder in her eyes: How do you clean that big, beautiful body?

Hailey: I know. She's like a dinosaur!

you're not a ballerina, Dadda
you're a King.

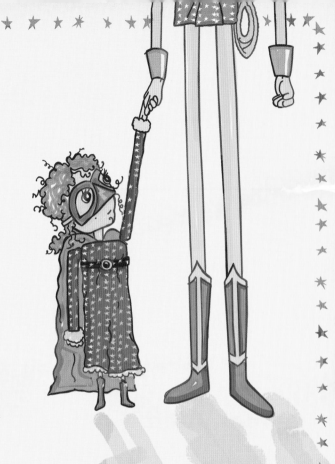

YOU'RE NOT A WOMAN, Mama.
YOU'RE A SUPERWOMAN...
AND I'M A SUPERWOMAN TOO.

Now it's YOUR turn!

Here's space to write down the funniest, weirdest, and most adorable quotes from your own kid:

....

....

....

....

....

....

....

....

....

....

Eternal gratitude to . . .

Michelle, for the countless hours of blood, sweat, and tears you put into helping me through this journey. I love you.

Harper, without you, none of this exists. I love you, too!

All of my family, especially Tom and Mary Bruckner, Mike and Connie Cartwright, and my grandpa Leo Widhalm—your doodles inspired my life.

My childhood art teacher, Peg Timmer-Kathol.

Jeff Wysaski of Pleated Jeans.

John LaRue, for always helping me when I was stuck.

Andrea Caniglia-Sayers and Lacey Sayers, for getting us our first quote book for Harper.

The awesome Oh-K Fast Print of Omaha, Nebraska.

My agent, Kirby Kim.

My incredible editor, Liz Davis, and Workman Publishing, for the opportunity of a lifetime!

And to every amazing family that has contacted me and trusted me to create a piece of artwork based on the special moments in your lives—thank you, it's been an honor.

About the Author

Martin Bruckner is a creative director, art lover, and lifelong artist.

When he was five years old and growing up in Norfolk, Nebraska, his favorite things in life were drawing and dancing with his mom. He and his mom had a very special song: "Could I Have This Dance (for the Rest of My Life)?" by Anne Murray. Anytime this song came on, they would dance together, but before they did, Martin would always approach his mom, bow his head, and say: "Could I have this dance?"

Martin now lives in Omaha, Nebraska, with his wife, Michelle, their daughter, Harper Grace, and their two dogs. Life is still filled with drawing and dancing, only now it's with his five-year-old daughter.

could I have this dance
for the rest of my Life?